THE ULTIMATE GUIDE TO SUCCESSFUL LEAN TRANSFORMATION

Top Reasons Why Companies Fail to Achieve and Sustain Excellence through Lean Improvement

Copyright © 2020 Mohammed Soliman

All rights reserved

Mohammed Hamed Ahmed Soliman

ISBN-13: 9798574453339

Contents

Introduction 4

Distinction between Lean Leadership and Classic Management Approach 7

Recruiting the Right Habits 22

Developing the Right Behavior 30

Motivating the Right Behavior 48

Strategic Alignment 55

Embedding Improvement into the Day 59

The Use of Cost Benefit Analysis in Decision Making 76

Switching to Lean Accounting 85

What is behind Success? 101

Appendix. I: Toyota Production System Critical Points 104

Appendix II. Lean Resources 119

References 122

About the Author 127

Also by Mohammed Hamed Ahmed Soliman 129

.... 129

Introduction

Many companies are complaining that lean didn't achieve their long-term goals, and the improvement impact was very short-lived. 7 out of each 10 lean projects fail as companies try to use lean like a toolkit, copying and pasting the techniques without trying to adapt the employee's culture, manage the improvement process, sustain the results, and develop their leaders. When the Toyota production system was created, the main goal was to remove wastes from the shop floor using some lean techniques and tools. What was not clear is that this required from Toyota a long process of leadership development, and a high commitment to training and coaching their employee. A Failure to achieve and sustain the improvement is a problem of both management and leadership as well as the improper understanding of the human behavior, and the required culture to success.

Throughout the years, lean leaders have become experts at improving processes. But in most cases, that's only a half-step. True lean leadership involves coaching and training your people so the improved process doesn't slip back from the ideal state, and the plan-do-check-act cycle is a remarkable tool for teaching.

The Toyota Way is held up by two main pillars: Continuous improvement and respect for people. And the good industrial manager knows that respect for people, which is about coaching, developing, supporting and valuing the workforce, is the foundation of continuous improvement.

Actually, people are more important than the process, and companies that put process before people will not earn sustainable results. People are the ones who build, operate, modify and improve the process. Therefore, developing people should be your company's highest priority. Focusing only on the process often will lead to system failure.

Early on, Taiichi Ohno, co-developer of the Toyota Production System, refused to document or write the system down for fear that people would focus narrowly on the tools and the theories. When he finally wrote it down, it was presented as a house because a house is a system. If you take away any of the structures that hold up the roof, the roof and entire system will collapse. One of Ohno's students said Toyota made a mistake calling it the Toyota Production System. Instead, Toyota should have called it the Thinking Production System because the real point was to make people think, and people are the value of the system.

Distinction between Lean Leadership and Classic Management Approach

Unfortunately, while many companies say that they value their people, they actually focus more on the process when using methodologies such as lean or Six Sigma. To develop a culture of improvement, you have to continuously coach and develop your people to change their habits, making improvement a routine.

In a classic management environment, managers who don't get results put pressure on their employees and push improvements. They are seeking quick results and short-term financial gain, not the long-term viable health of the organization. In bureaucratic management, managers take targets from the top and cascade them down to their workers, continually evaluating people using metrics. The ones who get the results are rewarded. The ones who fail might be punished.

Such leaders often are working to a financial plan, with the only care being climbing ladders rapidly and getting results at any cost. This is a classic example of managing people. And such leaders are separated from the reality of work because they don't take gemba walks to figure out what is really happening on the front lines.

On the other hand, the lean leader takes the target, breaks it down into manageable pieces and goes to the gemba to train, develop, improve and apply the method. This leader works horizontally to align the effort, method and plan across different functional departments with the company's business goal. This leader is seeking sustainable results. He works with people to solve problems. He goes to the gemba to learn deeply, develop himself and help others to learn and see. This leader is seeking the right process to get the right results by developing people through process improvement.

In the bureaucratic management system, people tend to hide their problems for fear of being blamed. This creates a dysfunctional culture unlike lean, which encourages problems to surface so they can be solved. Unfortunately, bad management habits will develop a negative culture that will continue to prevent organizational success.

MBO	Industrial Management using Hoshin Kanri for direction planning and deployment
Invented by Peter Drucker 1954	Originated in Japan in 1961 and used successfully by Toyota and top-tier companies in US and Japan
Management based on command and control	Management is based on empowering, motivating, and developing people on problems solving skills

Focus on the results	Focus on the process not the results this include the plan, the method, the innovation, and people development & training on problems solving
Recognize individuals	Rewarding system is based on teamwork, overall performance and accomplishments
Promote individualism	Promote teamwork
Top-down method	Top-down with linkage to shop floor
Managing process via distance and rely on reported metrics	Managing on shop floor (gemba principle) and base management decisions on facts

Use metrics to evaluate people and results	Give people degree of autonomy and use metrics to monitor the work progress and understand the obstacles need to be removed to improve the process.
Focus on the strategic thinking only	Link the strategic thinking to shop floor, use gemba as a management principle, and use visualization, standardization to improve the work

MBO was first presented by Drucker (1954). MBO is considered a method of planning and control to achieve the quantitative results. The method is also called management by results MBR.

The approach involves setting some objectives along with an incentive program in order to achieve the business goals.

Unfortunately, such an approach and the other management techniques are still being taught in many business schools neglecting the bad habits of the modern management and making the lean journey harder.

Indeed, there are many ways to achieve the quantitative targets without making real improvement. The MBO method may have worked in the earlier decades when the market condition was different. Now with the world events necessitating the reduction in wastes and maximizing the efficiency, the demand for real improvement has been increased.

For example, "10 percent cost reduction." Actually, there are many ways to reach this target, either by cutting some resources or improving the way of doing things. In the first option, you want to achieve a quick reduction and remain the same at what you are doing, in the second option you are searching for obviously perfection for longer-term financial benefit.

In MBO, since the objectives are focused on specific results the business needs, the top management sends this message to the down: "here is what we need and how your performance will be judged-go do your jobs and bring back the results whatever it takes." Metrics are used to measure the results, and control the employee rather than being a tool with the employee themselves to measure their own work progress. There are often some rewards for those who met the challenge. MBO ignores how the objectives are achieved as long as the results are got. What could make things harder are those bad managers who go aggressive in order to achieve the objectives putting pressure on people and pushing them to get quick results. And who failed to succeed may be downgraded position, punished, or left with no promotion. Some managers still have the sink or swim mentality. Those who find a way to succeed gets rewarded, others will let go.

Worse, the goals that have been set with MBO are magical goals that don't match the real state of the company. The senior managers who defined the goals have not been at the gemba before, so they are not aware of the real situation at the processes.

Gemba is the place where the value-creating work happens. It means go and see where the work is done to better understand the process and grasp the real situation. It also presents the Toyota way of developing their leaders. Toyota uses a parallel process called Hoshin Kanri for setting the targets and planning the achievement. Leaders, managers, and senior managers who have spent enough time at the gemba are contributed in the process of setting the company's goals. The company's vision, goals, and plans must be aligned for continuous improvement. Actually, the targets-setting process and the pursuit of targets cannot be independent, and it is far too focused on results without having a real understand of the means to get there. Also before seeking for accomplishments and results, leaders should be developed patiently through a long training process to insure that everyone has a deep understand about the process so he can turn those challenging objectives into an action plan to get stable results. The company's goals should be set and cascaded down to all levels to specific plans (means). A specific goal at the top management may have a different name at the operational level. For example, increasing the market share as a long-term vision specified at the top may require an increase of the quality at the down in the manufacturing process. Hoshin Kanri is an open mind method. It looks for the innovative ways of achieving the goals and focuses on developing and coaching people on problems solving. Hoshin Kanri is not just a management by both means and results. It also works under a self-development and a high motivated system.

Many companies are thinking that MBO as a tool is not a problem, but what is MBO as a tool? It is the managers making decisions about what they believe the business needs to go and turning those into objectives for their people. Sometimes objectives are being discussed among group of peoples, but often they are handed down from the top down. Since the focus is on the results only, there are many lost opportunities. MBO ignores the team orientation, the coaching process, the action plans, and the process of setting the goals which should be done by the leaders who know the real state of the company at all levels.

A good process of setting and planning the achievements will continually produce good results. A bad process might temporary produce the results under the pressure of managers but things will slip back again. Actually, people should be respected and treated like partners in the business. They should believe in the power of the system and that they are doing this for their jobs to become easier. Also if people are left to do the job without direct coaching and learning to maintain sustainability and achieve stable results, they will not feel about the power of the system. Executives who want to get the results without any of this and they have failed and must start over to develop appropriate leader skills.

Some companies use a culture of blame upon failure, this drive people to hide problems and present only what is good. Also imagine an organization full of people blaming, complaining, justifying, defending, and building cases against others, when would the work get done?

Therefore, managers should manage the process not the results, act as facilitators not blamers, and pay attention to how the goals are achieved not just the metrics.

A few steps to be considered for a successful process of setting, aligning, and achieving the objectives, (Ahmed, 2013):

- Establish a long-term reasonable vision based on what business needs and the current situation. Vision should be actionable, measurable, applicable, and have a time frame for achievement. It should match the current state of the company and the situation at the processes. However, some companies, and in crisis situations may find that using a long-term vision is useless. A 10-years vision wouldn't mean much if a company didn't exist in 12 months.

So targets should be set and adapted according to the real situation in order to help the company to survive and quickly bring the system to life.
- Senior managers, leaders at all levels, and those who have spent enough time at the gemba are those who should be involved in the process of setting the company's goals. They know how the work actually gets done and what opportunities for improvement available out there.
- Vision and goals should be shared with everyone in the organization, and cascaded down at all levels. Everyone must understand the goals and the intention behind them.
- Ensure people are trained enough to achieve the results appropriately. People should understand exactly what improvement is needed to achieve the results.

- At any organization, establishing a process like Hoshin Kanri or similar for setting and achieving the targets should be carried after the training and developing process to ensure that leaders are capable of taking challenge and managing the continuous improvement culture through the P-D-C-A cycle.
- Goals can be broken down into manageable pieces or few small targets in order to ensure the quality of implementation. It is good to slowly apply the P-D-C-A cycle at every step taken toward the next target, and remove the obstacles as find. It is not favorable to apply a large improvement at once. If there are some obstacles there, the resistance would be huge and the process will fail. There is always an unclear territory that hides many obstacles; this would never be

discovered unless we move forward to the next target and apply the continuous improvement cycle at every step taken.
- How are you managing to get there? This is the method of achieving the targets, it calls target means (plan). For each target the current condition should be specified as well as the target condition using the appropriated metric. In many conditions, setting a long term plan for making improvement and try to follow it is like moving in a road full of fog, if goals are broken to small targets, they would become easier to manage. There should be a plan for reaching each target. The next plan will be set for the next target according to the progress and the accomplishments.
- Train leaders on problems solving. This is one of the most critical

requirements to achieve the targets and remove the obstacles. Most of companies that fail to make real improvement and achieve good results have neglected the training and coaching as a necessary part of the process. Managers should dig deep in the details to discover root causes rather than jumping to solutions and the "do" phase in the continuous improvement cycle.

Recruiting the Right Habits

One of the initial steps for business success is getting the right people on the board with the appropriate skills and attitudes. How companies choose and hire their people reflect their organizational culture. These hires are going to develop new methods of working, invent new products, lead the transformation and build a successful business. They are the company's future leaders.

But do companies really get what they expect from their hiring candidates?

Traditionally, companies demand degrees and certifications to demonstrate expertise, while others prefer to hire based on experience, history and skills. Neither way will work if the organization in question refuses to develop a culture of improvement. Managers hire MBAs and Six Sigma black belts with the mistaken notion that they will transform the business without a transformation of management.

Yet what can a certificate holder do in a system that doesn't engage employees in the continuous improvement cycle, value their ideas and develop them continuously? A closer look at these companies reveals that they don't have a real system capable of utilizing and aligning employee skills and efforts to solve problems and achieve business goals. Your entire professional force can get certified, but if the company culture doesn't allow it, they won't get the chance to practice what they have learned.

And while certificates can prove ability, actual improvement will not occur without a high commitment to self-education and self-development to keep the certificate holder's knowledge up to date, allowing the person to develop better ways of working and practicing. Certificates don't drive performance competency in the practical world.

Josh Kaufman, author of international best-seller *Personal MBA*, wrote that a large body of evidence suggests that what some business schools teach has no connection to what is required for business success.

Unfortunately, according to Kaufman, many business programs have de-emphasized value creation and operations in favor of finance and quantitative analysis.

This extreme focus on financial analysis produces executives who are not capable of improving business performance, driving success and creating value for customers. It doesn't build distinguished leadership.

Reinforced by their MBA education, many executives and managers seek solid financial outcomes, although in many instances they have lost connection with the reality that exists on their organization's front lines. Decision-makers are poorly informed about the actual situation, and decision-making is based on incorrect assumptions and inappropriate targets. They have learned to manage the process via distance using some reported metrics. They have not been taught the culture of improvement.

For example, if managers remain behind the scenes and avoid actual place where the work is done (the gemba), they will not realize what small issues pop up as obstacles to success. They will make poor decisions. Then, when their business processes fail, the human resources department asks what went wrong. After all, they have hired professional qualified persons.

But hiring professionals won't, by itself, turn around an organization. However, having a real continuous improvement system and an embedded culture of improvement will. A system that empowers employees to make changes, motivates them in the right way, aligns goals and efforts with organizational strategies and vision, develops leaders continuously, bases management decisions on real situations, and makes improvement a part of everyone's daily routine is a system with a high chance of success.

Better questions, better results

When organizations base their hiring processes on certifications and classic interviews, what do the companies really know about these individuals, their behaviors and their openness to change? Do companies really get the results they need?

The hiring process can be improved to select better candidates if the human resources department, instead of asking for certifications, tests individuals properly and assesses their skills.

Toyota thinks approaches the hiring process differently. The powerhouse Japanese automaker wants to hire people who are motivated and highly committed to self-development and self-education. For Toyota to exceed customer expectations, its employees must do the same. Toyota tends to assess what its candidates know and how they are going to use that knowledge.

Jeffrey K. Liker's *The Toyota Way to Lean Leadership* originally reported that when Toyota started to hire leaders for the New United Motor Manufacturing Inc. (NUMMI) plant, the first joint venture plant between Toyota and General Motors, the focus was on hiring candidates who had demonstrated an inherent capacity for self-development and learning. Toyota wanted people who had an openness and excitement to learning new things.

Toyota also uses a system to test individuals for their abilities to work in a team. A group of candidates is placed in a meeting room and assigned a problem to solve. Toyota likes to hire the candidates who demonstrate the ability to function well in a team and devise a solution by working with others.

Organizations should use behavior-based tests and real assessments as part of any recruitment strategy. And this is where the application of industrial and organization psychology comes in.

In the book *Social Psychology and Human Nature*, authors Roy F. Baumeister and Brad J. Bushman reported that most companies use informal and unstructured behavioral interview questions like the following:

- What are your weaknesses?
- Why should we hire you?
- Why do you want to work here?
- What are your goals?
- Why are you leaving your job?

- When were you most satisfied in your job?
- What can you do for us that other candidates can't?
- What are three positive things your last boss can say about you?
- What salary are you seeking?

According to many psychologists and researchers, such traditional questions don't serve a company's real needs. Improving the hiring process to help generate a culture of change would involve using relative, reasonable and structured behavior questions such as these:

- Tell me in specific detail about a time when you had to deal with a difficult customer.
- Give me an example of a time when you had to make a decision without a supervisor present.
- Give me a specific example when you demonstrated an initiative in an employment setting.

- Give me an example of a time when you had to work in a team.
- Describe a time when you had to be creative at solving a problem.

Such questions tend to assess leadership and problem-solving skills, which is what most companies really need anyway.

Developing the Right Behavior

Toyota uses improvement kata to develop a routine that will systematic continuous improvement into all processes. And Toyota uses the coaching kata to coach people on the continuous improvement process so they are capable of meeting the targets and facing the challenge. The early stages of the improvement kata should be practiced under the watching eye of the mentor. So what makes good leaders?

Committing to self-development
Toyota hires people who are committed to self-development and openness to change. You simply can't force people to learn if they don't want to. You can force them to take notes and give feedback, but psychological experiments have proved that such learning will remain at a superficial level.

If only a few people in your system know how to solve problems, one of them leaving will disrupt the whole system. So your organizational target should be that everyone must learn and act. A company is strong because of its people, not its processes. And you have to standardize the learning process so it becomes a routine.

While people who are doing the work should be trained to improve the process, the real change always come from the top. For example, examine the New United Motor Manufacturing Inc.'s NUMMI plant, the first joint venture between General Motors and Toyota. The initial aim of the Japanese was to train plant manager Gary L. Convis. Convis was in the most critical position. Training him was the key to then training everybody in the hierarchy. Then training could move down to team leaders.

While teaching comes from the top to bottom, a company's decision-makers are the ones who can transform the organization. So ideally they would learn first. Of course, depending upon where you are in your corporate hierarchy, it could be difficult to persuade top management to visit the gemba regularly and get involved directly in the system's continuous improvement. If that's the case, training can start with the middle managers, supervisors and workers, who can select a small project to improve. Hopefully, early successes will convince top management of the importance of continuous improvement methodologies.

Learning to Lead at the Gemba
Few leaders go the gemba regularly. Some visit only when there is a problem. Others practice daily walks to observe people. To be a truly great leader, you have to learn how to lead at the gemba.

Gemba is the place where the value creating work happens. The real value from these visits comes from observing the actual situation at the processes, providing the needed support for the working teams, realizing what the actual situation is, making decisions based on facts instead of reported metrics, finding the root causes of the problems, improving the process, coaching people and improving people's safety and morale. Every lean tool that creates value and eliminates waste, from work standardization to value stream mapping, should be planned, applied, improved, adapted and standardized at the gemba.

Gemba walks should be one of the main core values for any company that wants to develop good lean leaders.

When Toyota hires new managers or leaders, they are expected to spend enough time at the gemba to understand the process and gain the trust of the people. In other companies, the spent at the gemba varies.

For example, when Convis was asked to leave the NUMMI plant and become president of Toyota's Kentucky plant (he was the first American to become president of that plant), Toyota told him that he would first have to learn the culture, get involved in the work and get his hands dirty to prove he could handle becoming president. He was to go to the gemba to learn the jobs, understand the people and understand Toyota. Convis had a year to accomplish this. In most corporate cultures outside of the Toyota group of companies, it is unusual for a president to spend so much time at the gemba.

Japanese culture believes in what they call t-leadership, where you should become an expert in a particular technical area before moving to the next level. You have to know what people are doing before you can lead them. When you become expert in something, you can start learning the basics of other things but you may not going to have the same depth of knowledge in the other fields and you are going to relay on other experts in these fields.

As Jeffrey K. Liker, author of *The Toyota Way to Lean Leadership*, explained, Toyota develops t-leaders by moving those with high potential first up the chain of command in their specialty. Then such leaders can move horizontally to different specialties. This also teaches leaders to manage vertically and horizontally. Leading horizontally across organizations is important when trying to solve large problems that cross different functional departments.

In far too many industrial organizations, CEOs have no idea about the many different operations that include the supply chain, production, quality and the culture of improvement. How do you expect to manage an organization when you don't understand the processes? Such managers cannot solve problems across different functional departments if they have never been at the gemba in those departments.

Learning by teaching and developing others

Companies are made of people, and people are not perfect. So continuously developing leaders is the key for perfection, which should be an ultimate goal. When Toyota develops a leader, that leader is expected to become a teacher and develop another leader. It is fundamentally a coaching cycle and a one-to-one coaching method.

For leaders to become coaches, they must be able to assess the trainee skills objectively and find the gap between the skills the trainee has and the skills the trainee needs. Discover the trainee's strengths and weaknesses and then begin coaching. Avoid giving detailed instructions or pointing out the solution. Instead, as Mike Rother presented in *Toyota Kata*, ask questions to observe how the mentee is thinking.

Leadership development is a practical, problem-solving process. Any classroom time should be short, brief and only for the purpose of providing an awareness level. Classrooms don't lead to culture change, but training leaders at the gemba will. Mentees will only learn by doing, and they must practice on a real project. The sha hi ri model of learning detailed below is a good starting routine.

The leader must build trust with the student. If you aren't trusted as a mentor and coach, I won't follow your lessons. In Japan, as Liker explained in *Developing Lean Leaders at All Levels*, the master rarely praises the student. However, this culture didn't work very well with Americans in the Toyota plants. Therefore, Liker wrote, the Japanese conclude that every criticism should include three things that are positive.

The lesson here is that you can't coach everyone and every culture the same way. Your coaching model must adapt. But the principles are always the same. Critical feedback can be important because without it, mentees won't know what to learn to improve for the next time. Yet a cascade of positive comments might lead the trainees to think that they are the best and need to learn nothing.

Shu ha ri is a model of learning that comes from the martial arts presented by Liker and Convis in his *The Toyota Way to Lean Leadership*.

Shu means to protect, and in this phase, students are being coached on the fundamentals under the eye of the master. Students must embrace the routine and copy exactly what the master is telling them. There is no deviation accepted.

Ha means to break away, and in this phase, after the student has learned these routines and the basics have become natural, the student has more freedom to practice unsupervised and diverge from these rules. The master may check on the student, who can apply the rules creatively but still must follow the standard rigidly.

Ri means freedom, and in this phase, rules and behaviors have become so ingrained that the student no longer thinks about them consciously. Students then are in the position to develop their own understanding. The student is working beyond the rules.

Think about the work standard. A worker has to learn how to assemble parts onsite following the standard work procedures strictly. The student will learn by doing. In the shu stage, the student will see how the work is done and try to follow the teacher. The worker will practice the job continuously until he or she reaches the second step, ha. The teacher will keep monitoring the student until he or she reaches the final stage, ri. At that point, the worker can observe the overall working procedures and take the responsibility to improve it.

Turning PDCA into a learning cycle
Mistakenly, many people think plan-do-check-act (PDCA) is a continuous improvement cycle, even if they neglect the human part. PDCA does aim to improve the process, but if you have only improved the process without developing and teaching your people, you have put the process at risk of slipping back.

People must be trained in the culture of continuous improvement so they can keep managing the process with the new method. PDCA is actually a remarkable learning cycle because people learn by doing. The best thing is to pick up a real project and start improving a process. You don't learn to play football by watching a game or golf by watching the coach. You have to practice under the watchful eye of the mentor to develop new habits and change the bad ones. An attentive coach is critical to helping you make a new method become routine.

Toyota has several steps in its problem-solving process, steps that cycle through the famous PDCA wheel.

1. Define the problem relative to the ideal (plan).
2. Grasp the current situation.
3. Break down the problem into manageable pieces (plan).
4. Find the root cause of the problem (plan).
5. Develop countermeasures (plan).
6. Implement the solution (do).
7. Examine what the actual outcomes are (check).
8. Adapt, adjust, standardize and scale the solutions to other areas (act).

Note that the plan phase is invoked five times before proceeding to the do phase. This is to ensure both the quality of the implementation and that the selected countermeasure will solve the problem. Lean emphasizes the plan. And the plan phase cannot be created without a daily observation at the gemba to find the root causes, gather facts, discuss things with the process operators and develop the best countermeasure from different alternatives.

Unfortunately, many leaders jump into the do phase without spending enough time observing the situation to find the real problem. The most enjoyable part for the leader is the "do," but jumping to the do usually results in a quick fix that not only might not solve the real problem, it could create wastes in other linked areas.

Jumping to the do phase can escalate the problem. Take the example of electrical problems in automobiles. In this case, the technician decided that the problem was in the spark plug coils pack. Changing that costs $350 dollar. Unfortunately, that wasn't the problem – a faulty engine control unit (ECU) was. Replacing the ECU cost $1,500. The waste in time, effort and resources led to a total cost of $1,850.

Define the problem relative to the ideal to find the current and ideal states. You might consider your quality ratio of 97 percent good, but any gap between the current state and what could be reached is an opportunity for your competitors. One of the main failures in this step is how people hide their problems because they fear blame. There is no culture of visualizing problems and surfacing issues. This always makes it difficult to define the problem and discover the gap between the current state and the ideal state.

Grasping the current situation is critical. Management decisions should be based on facts, not simply metrics or computerized reports. This is why it's so important for managers to go the gemba to see what reality is. Watch the process and look to solve the problem, and remember not <u>to</u> blame the people.

Break down the problem into manageable pieces. We have seen many companies set targets and cascade them down to the bottom levels. The leaders below are responsible for achieving this target in a timely manner. Top management may blame leaders if this target has not been achieved on time. Upper management also often sets too big of a target, such as an 80 percent improvement in quality improvement this year instead of 20 percent improvement for four years.

This is another example of poor management habits. Psychological experiments have proved that people tend to make progress on concrete, small goals rather than complex, large ones. Seeking large improvements at once will cause a system failure, especially when people are new to process improvement. Leaders have to be patient. Breaking down the target into small increments will encourage people to participate and act.

When searching for the root cause of the problem, remember that at first glance the problem can appear to be a person. But leaders have to dig deeper to find the true root cause. Overconfidence is one of the biggest barriers to problem-solving. Leaders think they know how to fix things and will follow the problem-solving process at a superficial level. Without the true root case, you probably will build a plan and invest in resources for something that is not going to work.

Select the suitable solution from different countermeasures that you have received from people involved in the process and from different perspectives. Lean encourages selecting a solution from different alternatives. Prioritize your options and select the countermeasure that has the highest chance of success. Perhaps you can choose one that is easier to try and relatively inexpensive. Then you have to develop your plan on who, when and where.

However, it is possible that spending time in the plan phase will not reveal the proper solution. At this point, a small pilot project might be necessary in an attempt to reveal the appropriate countermeasures.

Only then can you go to the "do" phase and implement the countermeasures. Be careful, as many managers think that this phase is the end of the issue, and once they pushed the button the system will go live and run forever. Keeping the process monitored is necessary. Continue coaching and supporting people to avoid slipping back.

You should also use metrics and post them in the workplace. This helps align people to common targets. Those metrics should be visualized in the workplace using visual boards. Later, the progress should be updated and discussed regularly. Use colors for in-progress targets and for the achieved targets. The metrics give a starting point to your workforce. What is our measurable target? Where are we? Where do we want to be?

In the "check" phase, remember that after implementing the solution, people will not always continue in the same way as you wished. They won't follow the standard all the time. Supporting people, continuously motioning them, coaching them and developing them until the new way becomes a routine is the key to a perfect solution. You may not achieve this in the first PDCA cycle. So you have to repeat it continuously and keep supporting people until the new standardized process becomes a routine.

The "act" phase is where the start of the next cycle begins. You next plan will be based on the feedback you received from the "check" stage. In this phase you, should figure out what did work, what didn't and standardize what worked.

Why develop people?

After the Toyota recall crisis several years ago, company President Akio Toyoda was quoted as saying that the corporation's rate of growth was higher its rate of people development.

The key success of Toyota's continuous improvement process is the effort that managers or leaders put in people development through the PDCA cycle. It is a remarkable learning cycle. As you go through each PDCA, you will learn different and higher levels of skills. This should be done under the eye of the mentor. Practicing new behaviors will shift the employees out of their existing routine and, over time, influence people's thoughts and actions. In the long term, repeated new habits can lead to a culture of continuous improvement. People should follow plan-do-check-act so often that it becomes natural way of thinking.

If a problem crops up that you thought had been solved, the proper question would be have you rotated the PDCA wheels enough times? PDCA needs to spin a lot before you reach your target, achieve a stable process and form new habits.

Motivating the Right Behavior

Taylor (1911) quoted "if each employee's compensation was linked to their output, their productivity would go up."

Normally, employees get paid to do their jobs. Salaries and other financial benefits are initially adapted to meet the employee satisfaction and the minimum expectation of the job role. Everyone will have a salary increase upon promoting position which depends on many things like proven of good leadership capability.

Lots of companies are using a reward system that is tied to specific metrics. Such a system can encourage individual behavior rather than a team orientation if not adapted properly. Everyone will strive to do the improvement for himself in the particular process he is managing to quickly get the results ignoring the overall performance of the plant and the real problem solving process. There will be no permanent solution for the chronic problems as problems solving requires a team cooperation in order to set the countermeasures, remove the obstacles, and implement the plan.

For example, in a company, a 20% from the employees monthly salary was cut and paid back to each one based on the accomplishments and the individual performance. The evaluation was being carried every 6 months and based on the measurable results outputted from each employee using some metrics. One of those targets for 2012 was to map certain processes and achieve numeric improvement in the value-added work for each process. One engineer from the working team commented to his leader: "frankly, we are going to get to you only what you need because this is how we get evaluated, but we can't guarantee the sustaining of this improvement unless the team members at the operation level are coached on how to properly do their job with the new way."

In Japan Toyota try to avoid tying specific rewards to specific metrics, fearing that employee would focus narrowly on what is measured and ignore the other parts of the job. Liker (2012) quoted "Psychological experiments show that paying people to do something that they already want to do either because they enjoy it or because they want to get good at it can kill the intrinsic motivation." The company will have to continually provide rewards if it wants to continue to see good behavior.

While Taylor focus on individual incentives based on productivity, Toyota focus on team working and the evaluation is based on the group performance.

However, this is not to say that incentives should not be used at all. The incentives can still be based on team working, large accomplishments, and the plant performance. But it should not be tied to individual accomplishments.

Also there are some morale motives that can reduce the demand of providing incentives such as: granting a certificate of appreciation to those who prove good things and good leadership capability, perform coaching and training and grant a certificate to those who pass the tests with remarkable results. Tests could be practical and real problem solving ones. And if employees are practicing what they learn, their learning experience will be increased through the implementation. Both the organization and the employees are getting a benefit from the system now. Also with coaching and certificating the successful, people will feel about the investment spent on them. The certificate can be useful for their future careers.

Using a certain promotion system is also a good motivation way. Those who prove a good leadership will be upgraded position.

Certainly, to success with lean, people should believe in the process and that they are doing the improving for their work to become easier, and safer not to get rewarded. They should be allowed to share and put their own ideas under a self-motivated and cooperative system to improve their own works. Also with a stable environment, the overall company's profitability will increase allowing more jobs for the labor force.

What to consider in a motivation system?

- Allow employee to share their own ideas for improving their own works. This will make the employee feel themselves and that they are valuable to the process. Employee should consider the improvement an enjoyable part of their work rather than a new method to follow. Giving people a degree of autonomy will increase the self-motivation.
- Use a certain system for promoting positions. Who will be promoted is who will prove good leadership and problem solving capabilities. Leaders who failed to meet the challenge or achieve the targets won't be punished, but will have fewer people reporting to them and may go through more training cycles.
- Senior leaders should act as mentors for the younger leaders. And younger leaders should develop the working teams. Such a training system will make better environment for learning and encourage self-development. People should learn how to improve

themselves continuously through practicing what they learn. In such a culture, the system will be appreciated by everyone. People learn more by doing, and then the practical improvement will increase their learning experience and meet the company's needs at the same time.
- People are most likely to make progress on goals that are broken into concrete, measurable actions, with some kind of structured accountability and positive reinforcement.
- Avoid incentives that are based on individual accomplishments and use awards for team accomplishments and plant performance. Japan's culture believes that there is no reason to incentivize exceptional performance when it is what is expected, however, with the other different cultures like America, Europe, Africa, there is a use of some rewards and a bonus system that is based on a group performance.

- If the organization has clear vital objectives that are separated into reachable goals, workers will have the option to create thoughts and clarify how their thoughts are lined up with these objectives. The framework itself will drive inspiration and innovation. There will no more be a requirement for budgetary sparks that undermine execution and murder inspiration. A framework that trains directors and designers to tune in to the laborers' issues and enables data to be shared between gatherings can be astoundingly persuasive (Balle and Balle, 2014).

Strategic Alignment

There is no reason to say that companies should not try to get rapid results with the implementation of lean in everywhere in the company and at every process. But this should be done without scarifying the learning. Culture adaptiveness and leaders development are very important in order to get sustainable results, otherwise, the improvement will be a short-lived one. All efforts, resources, and tools that have been spent to achieve the results will be lost.

Lots of companies tend to focus on improving as many individual processes as possible using a tool like VSM rather than focusing on the whole value stream. In the value stream you look at a series of processes together. This gives better results and ensures the quality of improvement. The focus on maximizing the efficiency and the capability of a single process can negatively affect another process. Processes shouldn't be improved at the expense of the others.

For example, one of the main lean goals is to make one piece flow through the production processes and minimize the work in process WIP inventory. If you are assembling one piece of product in 10 minutes, the wait to assemble 10 pieces and send them together in one large batch is 100 minutes, so the time of assembling one piece has become 100 minutes although the value added time is only 10 minutes. Moving one piece of product every 10 minutes will reduce the lead times of making the product, minimize the WIP inventory and speed up the delivery to the customer. But this can put load on the transportation process and increase the efforts especially when the process steps are not close to each other's. So improving the efficiency of the transportation process should be also considered. Producing with small batches may be a good compromise. And to continuously improve this process and provide one piece of product or reduce the batches size, you have to continuously improve the transportation too and eliminate all obstacles.

Although analyzing the whole value stream usually give good results over the analysis of the individual processes, but analyzing the individual processes and improving them can give quicker result. Usually, when analyzing a series of processes in the value stream there will be also a series of issues that are linked together. They will take much longer time to be improved and may need to be divided into small issues and each will go through the continuous improvement cycle P-D-C-A. This is not usually works when there are many companies out there that still don't believe about the workability of lean. In such a culture it is preferably to show quick results by looking at the processes that can be improved easily and quickly and avoid waiting to improve the overall value stream that will take longer time to fix. When the top management sees quick results from lean, they will provide the support needed for more improvement.

Value stream mapping VSM is a good lean tool that is being used to improve the process. A part from the fact that VSM is not exactly a tool for process improvement rather than a tool to insure that process improvement efforts:

- Fit together from a process to process so that a flowing value stream is developed.
- Match with the organization's targets and business needs.
- Serve the requirements of the external customers.

Some companies utilize the VSM to make improvement as found and perform random improvement for discovered wastes without having a clear vision that based on the current situation and the real business needs. It is better to perform VSM based on reasonable objectives and specific plans in order to reflect the change and improve the overall company's business process.

Embedding Improvement into the Day

In his book *Toyota Kata*, Mike Rother wrote that none outside of the Toyota group of companies has successfully brought systematic continuous improvement into all processes every day and across the organization. Even Toyota's efforts to spread its approach of continuous improvement to outside suppliers have not met expectations.

Truly, most organizations remain far away from establishing a solid continuous improvement system, and current management behavior rarely leads corporations to do what they should do in terms of both process and people management. Bad habits, behaviors done with little or no conscious thought, continue to affect culture and hold companies back from success.

Often, employees don't focus on improvement because of the lack of "north goals" and the improper alignment of departmental goals with the organization's strategies and vision.

In the Toyota vision, "north goals" refer to the long-term vision, such as being the best automotive maker in the world or holding more than 50 percent of the market share. In his book Toyota Kata Mike Rother calls the process of setting targets and striving toward them in Toyota the "improvement kata," and management focuses each day on coaching employees on how to reach those targets – targets that are aligned with the company's long-term vision.

A kata is a series of practice moves to build on form and technique. For our leaders, we want them to be able to do two things: Systematically improve processes toward a clear target (improvement kata) and coach others on the improvement kata (coaching kata).

Improvement kata really describes the Toyota habits for continuous improvement.

Toyota uses its improvement kata to make a way of a managing and working that we normally reserve for crisis situations. And the more often employees practice these new improvement behaviors, the more likely it will become a routine.

Concrete, stretch goals, aligned with organizational strategies, are the key to making improvement a priority. Stretch goals break down strategic goals into easy to understand bites that workers can digest and are a main way to cascade organizational values down from above to the front lines. For example, it means nothing to tell your employees that the goal is to be the leading supplier in the industry. But breaking that aim down into stretch goals yields metrics, such as "50 percent reduction in defects per year," or "20 percent productivity gain each year," that can measure results.

By repeating the continuous improvement cycle and using "smaller" stretch goals, organizations can achieve their long-term vision. Departmental goals should be aligned with the company's strategic objectives or the employees will wonder why they are bothering to improve the system. People tend to make progress on things they believe in. It is a part of any motivation program.

People should believe in the power of the system and that they are working to make their job and life easier and safer. The company's success is their success. This is where the intrinsic motivation comes from. If goals are not specified, people won't improve because they will think everything is fine.

But if the company has clear strategic goals, goals that are broken down into achievable metrics, employees will generate ideas and explain how their ideas are aligned with these goals. The system itself will drive the motivation and creativity of everyone. There will be no more need for financial motives that undermine performance and kill motivation. A system that trains supervisors and engineers to listen to the workers' problems and allows information can be exceptionally motivational.

When psychology gets in the way

Think of your vision in business terms – such as No. 1 market share, zero warranty cost and 100 percent accountability. Break those down into stretch goals for your employees and departments to use. Make sure these stretch goals are concrete and aligned with your strategic business objectives by aligning them with the value you provide to your customers.

Goals can't be things like standardizing the work process, which simply opens up the work force's psychology to a host of questions. The human mind always seems to latch on to criticism of change. Workers will wonder why they are standardizing the work. After all, they're OK with the current process. Why should we put forth energy and effort instead of focusing on a higher priority? If improvement doesn't have a clear direction and assigned priority, people will consider it low priority and continue with their current methods.

As explained in Toyota Kata, Toyota inserted continuous improvement into its employee DNA by using the kata approach.

Improvement became a part of each employee's daily routine, something that can't be achieved through formal trainings or classrooms.

Take, for example, the question "What do you want to do to improve your work?" The answer can be "We need to reduce setup times, apply a production pull system, remove wastes from the shop floor, reduce production lead-times and standardize work procedures." This is what most companies do, and it represents a poor alignment of goals with strategies.

Lean improvement, on the other hand, strives toward an objective. A better question would be "What is your target?" The answer could be "Meeting the customer demand rate (takt time)." This begs the question of what do the workers need to reach this target, which yields the answer that they need to improve the cycle time of their machines to meet the customer takt time.

The second case clearly defines customer takt time as a stretch goal to strive for. We know where we want to be. And improving machine cycle is a target condition that we must meet to reach our goal. It should be a measurable thing, like a cycle time of 50 seconds faster than the takt time. The first example has no target, and we could spin our wheels improving things while not knowing where we want to be or where this improvement will lead us.

One of the most fundamental mistakes made by many companies is trying to improve something without a clear strategy that serves the customer requirements and finally the success of the business. Definitely, meeting the customer demand rate will allow the organization to deliver products on time and achieve 100% customer satisfaction. This can serve the long term strategic objective of being a leading supplier.

People and core values

You will need a strategy statement that articulates your vision and incorporates the stretch goals that are required to achieve it. Even if your people don't fully understand where you are taking them, repeating the words of your strategy will help them understand that they are part of a team going in the same direction.

These statements should be generic enough that your vision will fit any future acquisitions. It is important that your strategy defines the operational excellence that you envision. For example, be the leading supplier in your industry or be one of the globe's top 10 corporations.

Core values must be articulated. Achieving excellence requires teamwork, trust and respect for people. Core values are like guideposts that will point your workforce toward your ultimate goal of working in a culture of improvement.

The three main core values to consider are people, customer and quality. Respect for people is one of the Toyota production system's pillars and is the main reason for Toyota's success.

A policy of not laying off employees because of improving efficiency is a good thing to follow. Letting workers go after they improve a process will disrupt the whole system, and it means no improvement in the next time. Employee will resist change as long as it threatens their livelihoods. If a strategy of respect for people is set, then a 20 percent cost reduction target clearly means process improvement, not cutting resources. Always remember that a company can't change its core values every few years without losing the respect and confidence of its people.

Respect for people includes developing your leaders instead of outsourcing solutions. Many companies hire external experts. They create a continuous improvement department, hire the improvement consultants and relegate the improvement behavior to them. Such a parallel team will be powerless to effect change and make improvement. They don't know the company's culture or processes.

But when the outsourcing consultant leaves, all knowledge is gone. The regular employees have no experience to keep managing the improved processes or continuously improving them to face the future challenges. They have not been trained on the culture of continuous improvement and have not contributed to the transformation process.

Instead, lean tools should be used by the company's leaders and the factory managers who have the capability, power and responsibility to effect changes.
Improvement should be done by people who are managing the work day by day, not by a parallel team. The leaders who manage work each day will be responsible for coaching people who do the work. And those people must own, operate, develop and continually improve their processes. Companies that travel the consultant route should make sure they use the temporary personnel to share lean expertise and knowledge with the rest of the workforce.

Classroom vs. continuous coaching

We learn by doing, and problems give us lessons to learn. What we learn through formal educational programs can't be standardized for all industries and cultures. What might work in one place won't work in another. Situations differ, even in the same industry. Anyway, classroom training, while it can only provide a specific level of awareness, does not change behaviors and culture.

Toyota uses a completely different pattern of learning. Toyota teaches its workers to develop solutions, not just to solve problems. The automaker's employees learn a routine of thinking and acting that harnesses the human capability to improve. Many companies aim to teach their employees skills, delegating the process to the training department or human resources. Those departments might assess what employees know, their performance, and train them accordingly.

Instead, as a commitment to self-education and continuous development, Toyota's kata system continuously develops people and ensures that each mentee has a mentor. For example, the team member is coached by the team leader, and the team leader is coached by the group leader. This is Toyota's method for passing its improvement kata on to all organization members.

Continuous coaching at the workplace builds strong leaders. Embedding this into the organization's daily routine will make improvement a habit of everyone. This is a main reason why continuous improvement becomes a behavior pattern for everyone in Toyota's organizations. The learning cycles that Toyota leaders have to take, the continuous coaching at the workplace, and the utilization of problems as an opportunity to learn and grow have made Toyota a remarkable company.

As Liker explained in *Toyota Under Fire*, this is what allowed Toyota to come out stronger after several recall crises in the 200s. It helped Toyota stand out during the global recession.

Toyota doesn't rely on certifications and formal education programs. In fact, Japanese business culture doesn't think much of such certifications and MBAs because management and leadership should be taught at the gemba, where the actual work is done. This is where Toyota and many other Japanese businesses conduct most of their training. Toyota's kata system is one of the best strategies ever created to learn and develop leaders. As Rother presented in

Toyota Kata, Toyota specifies, aligns, and achieves the outcome targets via the improvement kata behavior. This process removes obstacles and keeps repeating the plan-do-check-act (PDCA) cycle at every step. At the same time, Toyota's coaching kata coaches people on how to achieve their goals and meet target conditions. Toyota is teaching people across organization a behavior routine that aligns people and functions in accordance with the organization's philosophy and vision. It doesn't remove obstacles in the improvement journey, and it doesn't tell you how to do that. The classroom training provides a little inspiration and some ideas, but people must start thinking through their own problems to develop solutions.

Classroom trainings are very useful for providing initial awareness and information, but they do not lead to culture changes and they do not develop high-level leadership. I conduct classes at the American University in Cairo. The interactions between people with varying levels of knowledge and experiences from different industries can make those classroom lessons worthwhile. However, here are a few things classroom training does not do. However, here are a few things classroom training does not do:

1. It doesn't provide direct solutions—only awareness. It will not teach you how to solve problems. You have to develop your own method.
2. It doesn't bring motivation. A lot of business programs are still searching for the magic stimulus, but real motivation comes from the problems and challenges at the gemba. Certifications or educational degrees will not motivate people.
3. It doesn't change behaviors or habits. According to several research studies, classrooms do nothing to form new habits or change culture (Rother 2009).
4. It doesn't motivate people to make changes and get involved in the system's continuous improvement.

This is purely a leadership issue and a top management commitment.
5. It doesn't build exceptional leadership. Leaders have to go through several training cycles, and actual problems have to be utilized as opportunities to learn and grow. The T-leadership model is a good model to follow, and leaders must learn and teach management at the gemba.

What about your business?
Start with a vision. For struggling businesses, a long-term vision of five or 10 years won't mean much if the company ceases to exist in 12 months. In this case, targets should be adapted to match the real situation to help the company survive.

Goals can be broken down into more manageable pieces and smaller increments. This ensures quality implementation. You also can apply the PDCA cycle slowly at every step and remove obstacles as they are found. It is preferable not to apply a large improvement at once. The obstacles and resistance to such change would be huge, and the entire program could fail quickly.

For each target, specify the current condition and the target condition using the appropriate metric. In many conditions, setting and trying to follow a long-term plan for making improvements is like moving in a road full of fog. Breaking the goals into smaller, stretch targets make them easier to manage, motivating your workers to strive for success. Specify a plan for reaching each target, make it actionable and give it a time frame. Get your people involved in how to do it, and listen to their ideas carefully.

It is important not to neglect the training. Most companies that fail to reach their improvement goals have neglected the training and coaching, which are necessary parts of the process. Managers should dig deep in the details to discover root causes rather than jumping to solutions and the "do" phase in the continuous improvement cycle.

Changing cultures and breaking old habits is the key to better performance. Cultural behaviors drive competency, company growth and continual success. Organizations culture need change if they want to embed continuous improvement into everyone's daily routine.

It is easy to talk and hard to do. It requires long-term management support and internal investment. Practicing new behaviors will shift the employees out of the existing routine and, over time, influence people's thoughts and actions. In the long term, repeated new habits can lead to a culture of continuous improvement.

The Use of Cost Benefit Analysis in Decision Making

To overcome the global recession, some companies have cut resources and laid off workers, while others adopted better strategies to improve processes and change culture. Unfortunately, there remains a gap between successful and less successful companies in terms of process management, people management and the adaptability of culture. Culture drives competitive advantage in companies like Toyota, which has a psychology of process improvement unlike its competitors. Toyota's lessons can help other organizations change the routines of thinking and acting to teach employees how to improve.

Frequently, cost benefit analysis is being carried by those accountants and inexperienced estimators to determine the beneficial of the next step required in the lean improvement initiative.

For example, a common mistake made by many manufacturing is the arrangement of the machines by similarity rather than by the sequence of the process steps. This system hides many wastes behind it. The transportation cost will be increased allowing more resources to be used to transfer one piece of product from a process to another. There will be much WIP inventory buildup between the process steps and a process might have to wait until it gets the material it needs for work. This will affect the external customers, delay the product delivery, and affect the quality too.

Indeed, machines arrangement should take into consideration the following things: minimizing the WIP inventory, minimizing the time it takes to produce one piece of product, be faster than the takt time which is the customer demand rate for a product or group of products. And consider all workstations, machines, and operation tools to be as close as possible to avoid waiting for tools or parts issue and what is called ergonomics in the workplace.

Commonly, when a cost benefit analysis CBA is performed, the cost of re arranging the machines would be very high on the short-terms. But, the main lean goal is to make one piece flow, minimize the WIP inventory, and shorten the lead times which have proven to give remarkable results on the long-terms. So the CBA if considered over months, years, the cost of doing the job once and for all will be less than the cost of keeping the situation as it is with all the wastes. Also customer satisfaction and delivery speeds should be considered as customer are what keep any organization in business.

At this case, CBA can be carried to determine the best method that should be used to re arrange the machines not to decide whether to make it or not. Also the CBA can be useful to determine the speed of making the changeover.

Short-term focus on cost reduction

The traditional working environment often presents a lack of trustiness between the labors who are working at the down operation level and the managers who are working at the top management level. There is always a resistant between both. Managers treat labors like machines, over burden them to achieve the company's goals. The rule is: "extract the maximum for lowest fees." And labors try to preserve their jobs and use some tricks to keep working with their preferable method constraining any improvement.

Worse, if lean are being used as a resources reduction tool, no real improvement will be gained. As long as labors believe that lean and other improvement methods will make them lose their jobs, they will not buy-in. Apart from the fact that the lean savings would be meaningless in terms of savings when a company have a large excess in capacity, if a company decide then to lay off the people, all of the savings will be blamed on lean.

In a company that was driving a bad culture and remove labors after each improvement project. The labors have been heard saying: "last time we did this improvement half of us lost their jobs, we have to keep working as we are to preserve our jobs."

An industrial engineer at the same company was measuring the time it takes to complete a specific process using a stop watch and counting the time of each work step in order to develop a work standard procedure. Labors were noted using some tricks to expand the time it takes to complete each part of the work, making the lean job harder.

When a company decide to start the improvement process by eliminating wasted motions on the shop floor; this will lead to removal of workers from a line or cell, those workers should be placed on another job so less workers has to be hired in the future. What Toyota production system does it provides something to do with any extra regular employees; such as work in kaizen teams to improve on standardized work, improve downtimes, identify the root causes of quality problems and develop countermeasures, train more deeply in problem solving, and find better ways to move materials.

Generally, companies that want to build a good lean culture should avoid connecting the kaizen work to the layoff process. Some companies have realized this, so they tend to transfer the extra labor from one line to another or use them in elsewhere in the company to avoid the layoff.

To maintain good relation and a foundation of trust between the top management and the workers, a few gemba walks can be considered by managers that should include: watching the working environment to grasp if something is wrong that could affect the safety at the working area, monitor to see if operators are performing any unsafe act, monitor the working environment for further problems that are preventing labors from doing their jobs smoothly such as no tools available in place, no spare parts, delay in transportation of material, and the existence of unsafe equipment in the working area like forklifts, and give high priority and commitment to the workplace cleaning and organization (like doing 5S). With such a clean, safe, and comfortable environment, labors will feel that everyone in the company is committed to the employee safety and satisfaction as well as the improvement, and development of the working process to make things easier and not just the targets and accomplishments.

Workers must be treated like appreciated assets, and because process is being continuously improved by those who are involved directly in the operations under the leadership of the operation managers, so the value of those workers will be increasing time by time.

There are many lessons to learn from Japan Toyota. Liker and Convis (2012) expressed that Toyota responded to the crises of recalls and recession by doing more kaizen, and more self-development, and used the opportunity to build a more stable foundation for the future. Toyota didn't close any of its plants and didn't lay off the regular employee. Unfortunately, we see companies in the recession time's cut-costs and reduce wages and their first thinking would jump into pause any training process in order to reduce the overheads.

However, in crisis situations, some companies are forced to sell assets or layoff people in order to survive and avoid bankruptcy. What is mentioned is the culture that should be maintained in almost stable environments. Layoff should not be an easy tool and a normal habit for cost reduction. It has a very negative effect on companies that want to maintain a good culture and gain sustainability with lean. Actually, some companies have a very reactive culture and short-term focused. When the sales are down, they immediately put pressure on people to make them leaves in order to cut costs and keep the profitability at the same level.

Reinforced by their MBA educations, many executives and managers seek solid financial outcomes. In many instances, though, they have lost connection with the realities that exist on their organizations' front lines. Decision-makers are poorly informed about the actual situations, and decision-making is based on incorrect assumptions and inappropriate targets. They have not been taught the culture of improvement.

Switching to Lean Accounting

For the past decades, financial folks relied on old principles, techniques and theories in determining the performance of the companies and give feed backs to the executives and CEOs so they can make the necessary improvement and take decisions. The CEO wants help finding the resources to fund a new project; he wants to know where we can improve costs in products and services, and he wants to know whether improvements made have resulted in financial gain. The CEO needs help seeing where the company has improved or declined and what the future looks like given the current circumstances.

Unfortunately, many corporate management accounting systems are inadequate for today's environment. They haven't been improved substantially since then. A famous example of this is the use of

ABC (Activity Based Cost) system. *Jean E. Cunningham and Orest J. Fiume* indicated that many companies have found ABC encourages batch processing in order to spread costs over a larger number of units in favor of reducing the unit/cost.

In the unique book *Real Numbers by Jean E. Cunningham and Orest J. Fiume,* the authors presented how for decades US was the world's manufacturing giant, home of quality and efficiency. Many industrialists didn't notice until too late that they were getting clobbered in the marketplace. Especially in the automotive industry, giants like GM, Ford, and Chrysler were losing significant market share to Japanese companies, led by Toyota.

Because most of accounting systems were mostly developed in the early 1900s to support manufacturing products in batches, these same systems now send wrong, and sometimes disastrous signals in a lean environment. It is like an island in the stream, the accounting areas have remained rooted to the methods that have been taught in business schools for decades.

If you work in an accounting department, look at where your department is and where people go during the day. Do accountants come in, sit at their desk and remain fixed there all day long? Are they far from the rest of the action? Do they ever go to the site where parts are being purchased, where products are being designed? If they do not, if people from through the business have to come to accounting to seek information, it is a good indication that the accounting team is sidelined!

Current financial models

Companies that are moving rapidly to lean and seeking to continuously improve their processes will find that the current financial model is not working because most of financial models are based on large batches which is against lean production. Lean is based on making to order (Soliman, 2015).

A classic example is the use of EOQ & EPQ formulas

The terms Economic Order Quantity & Economic Production Quantity have been around for many years much longer than lean methodology and Just in Time. EOQ was first developed by F. W. Harris in 1915. The problem is that EOQ is an old term from the old days getting used in a new world in a new way. It doesn't take into account many of the hidden losses. The major problem with EOQ is that the model is viewed as static. Using Lean, the model changes with every improvement.

Unfortunately, EOQ is still being taught in many international business, financial, and cost management programs in the universities and in all over the world without considering the dramatic change made by lean and the transformation to the material movement methods. *Making Materials Flow by LEI* provide the necessary material calculations for the lean environment (Harris, 2003).

The most common problems that can be found in the current industrial accounting & cost accounting processes that need to be adequate are summarized here:

1. Financial thinking is still stuck on batch production

One clear example for this is keeping a piece of equipment running constantly utilized because accountant said this machine must run constantly to make it profitable and keep unit cost low. So company's buy materials it doesn't need, pay an operator to run parts that are not needed and puts unnecessary tear and wear on the machine. This is all done because accounting blessed the machine's purchase based on specific parameters, which included sales projections which were too optimistic (Ahmed, 2014).

In lean, if you don't need the parts, don't run the machine. The cost of resources spend to make unsellable products plus the cost of holding the inventory is greatly bigger than the cost of not utilizing the machines to their maximum capacity (Ahmed, 2014; Soliman, 2017).

2. Financial data arrives late and often misleading

When accountant deliver old news, what do we do with old news? Accountant in many instances spend a lot of time counting things and producing outdated reports while many of these costs can be easily expected and placed before the end of the month. If you want the information to be valued, don't give it to the executives after the activity is completed! In some cases, information is weeks late. In lean environment, immediate visual feedback is required in order to eliminate root causes and prevent problems from recurring to gain high competitive advantage with your business operations.

3. Matching
All costs to manufacturer the goods you sell must be recognized as an expense in the month you recognize the revenue. Most costs need to be recognized in the month they happen. A practical example: the materials that you bought for a product that will ship in two months will be kept as inventory on your balance sheet. It is not an expense until you ship the product. The cost of advertising that product, or any other, is recorded as an expense on the books in the month it happens. This has been the genesis of a lot of standard cost accounting techniques. In lean, as lead time shrinks, products that are being made should be shipped in the same month so there is an opportunity to simplify accounting procedures and produce meaningful reports.

4. Moving rapidly to automation
In many companies I have seen, switching to automation became a source of cost reduction. In many instances, this can be just a form of transferring the costs from one area to another (from Direct to Overhead).

Moving to automation without eliminating wastes is just like automating the wastes.

Taking the example of complex and expensive machines/lines that can combine several processes in one process, usually the cycle time of those machine slower than the cycle time of the other simple machines (cycle time is the time required to process one unit of product). Often those complex machines are not flexible in responding to the high increase in demand so you have to buy more expensive machines to expand your capacity if the demand was to increase.

At the other hand, if demand is decreased you are stuck with non-utilized expensive machines and this involve a high depreciation cost that you will have to pay independent of the production volume.

With the simple machines, they tend to cycle faster and usually perform fewer types of tasks/processes or only one process. They are better anyway in term of demand fluctuation. They can respond to demand increase or decrease more efficient and at lower costs.

Accountant also spend a lot of time trying to collect costs using bar codes and other modern methods. Without improving the process itself, using advanced technologies can became another source of money wasting.

5. Financial statements
When financial statements became difficult to understand they became not trustfully, because we don't trust what we don't understand. The reports must be presented in a manner that can be read and easily understood by non-accountants.

Unfortunately, some business programs have gone the route of teaching all people in a business how to understand the numbers. Companies create classes for their employees to help them understand the numbers. Would not it be easier to make the numbers understandable? Non-understandable reports, inefficient reports and late reports can be all classified as waste.

6. Performance reports

All companies attempt to establish metrics to determine if they are achieving their goals. Unfortunately, many of these measures are too complex for average worker to be actionable, and some create dysfunctional behavior.

Also there are many performance measures that you don't need or don't present the real state of the company. There are many other helpful measures that are available in the lean books and references which can be used to help executives make decisions.

Example, one of the business premier measures, stressed in most financial management programs and treated as one prevailing metric, is return on investment ROI, As currently practiced, ROI is an excellent example of the intent to capture many complex and interrelated events, thus creating one monster of a metric that few people can relate to their daily activities. ROI involve huge parameters and factors and should not be used as a standalone measurement and should not be used as the only measurement around. If everything is being counted in term of immediate or direct financial benefits, the indirect improvements to quality, down times and setups may not get the attention and the resources they deserve because everything is being evaluated in terms of financial benefit. Many direct financial metrics are not efficient in the modern environments and you have to develop your own ones and shift people's thinking so they can think more proactively in terms of company's success and customer. Liker (2003) quoted *"Base Your Management Decisions on a Long-Term Philosophy, Even at the Expense of Short-Term Financial Goals."*

7. Stuck with cost accounting rather than cost management

It is far less important to count the cost of making a product that it is to manage the cost of the whole business. Traditional cost accountant is dependent on establishing a standard method for calculating the cost of making every product and every component the company make. In most of companies, the accountant department is trying to figure out the best method of calculating costs rather than trying to manage, reduce and plan the cost of designing and making this product.

Most studies show that 80-95% of the life-cycle cost of a product is committed during the design process. That mean only 15-5% of the total cost is susceptible to future cost reduction effort without redesigning the product.

8. Budget planning

Every year we see financial guys negotiating for a tough budget and operations guys negotiating for an easy budget so they can look good. In the end, the financial guys own the budget. Operations can say "It is not my fault you gave me a bad budget" Often this creates a lot of conflicts between operations and accounting. Financial guys always wait until the end to provide an evaluation and judge the situation, then report what went wrong. Would not be better for them to begin with the planning process and offer help? *Chief Financial Officer, Greg Flint quoted "I don't think budgets are worth a hill of beans. They are based on guess work and politics."*

9. Accounting process and non-value adding activities

Many accountants spend time doing non-value added activities, record unnecessary information, produce unneeded data and duplicate things. Even the value added work they do may arrive late (the reports) so it became obsolete and outdated. There is no systematic method to produce on time reports to help track the root causes of issues. What have gone wrong have gone wrong, what is the purpose from keep recording it??!

I personally found many accounting systems contain waste. As with any other business process, accounting processes can be improved to eliminate waste and allow for timelier reporting of valuable information (lean accounting).

What should we do?
Sometimes improvement has been blocked due to barriers created by accounting. If managers didn't notice the effect of improvement on the company's performance, they won't support the idea or commit to the resources required. How many times have we heard executives say, "What you really do has no benefit to the organization? I don't know what you are doing, but whatever it is, stop it, you are killing profits."

Involve your account people in the change. If they are not involved in change, the will remain mired in the old culture, along with batch processing and standard cost accounting. Accountants are not just a report generator, they are business partners.

Accountants should switch themselves from focusing on transaction processing or bean counting to becoming valued business partners who contribute meaningful information for decision-making purposes.

The goal of accounting education
The goal of an accounting education is not to prepare for a life time recording debits

and credits, but to learn a language and tools to assist a business toward better performance.

As you continuously improve your process and make serious progress in the transition to lean manufacturing, you have to continuously improve the accounting method, keep accountant folks updated, educate them and get them involved in every step you make. This is to avoid the serious disconnect that will occur between the operations and accounting (Byrne, 2012).

What happened to cost management certification programs?

I personally hold a certification in cost management that is internationally accredited. And I'm pretty confident to say that it only served as start so you can begin thinking on how to improve the way things are being done in your organization. It didn't provide information on how lean accounting work or how to improve costs, just a background on how basically cost is being counted and planned so you can brainstorm where the defects are coming from. I got the knowledge through practicing lean and reading a lot of lean and continuous improvement references.

What is behind Success?

People must have degree of security and feel they belong to the team. Jobs must be designed to be challenging. People need some autonomy to feel they have control over the job. Nothing motivating as challenging the targets, constant measurement, and feedback on progress, and an occasional reward based on group accomplishments.

Although Toyota use its own business practice in defining strategies and goals, but there is no magical tool behind the Toyota success. Liker (2012) summarized six points to be made for any organization that wants to begin the lean journey:

1. There must be a shared vision that is believable actionable and reinforced in concrete terms as the work is done.

2. Developing leaders that are willing to take the challenge through self-develop, and keep coaching them at the gemba.

3. Turn the role of leaders from decision makers to teachers so they can develop the other leaders.

4. Developing a continuous improvement culture through the plan-do-check-act to continuously improve the processes. Spend enough time at the plan and check phases, and avoid rapid jump to act phase.

5. Aligning the targets and plans to achieve the results and use problems solving to remove the obstacles.

6. Using the major challenges from the environment to further strengthen the company and the leaders to work toward a long-term vision like the respond of Toyota to the crises of recall, recession and Japan earthquakes.

Toyota uses a very deep and patient process to develop their internal leaders. Even most of trainings are being carried at the gemba, and very few are carried in classrooms. The formal classroom training is ineffective alone for changing people behaviors. The process was expressed deeply by Rother (2009).

It has been verified that to build exceptional people and teams, this must derives from having in place some form of a "respect for humanity system."

Appendix. I: Toyota Production System Critical Points

What Toyota's Production System Is Really About?

Many people don't understand the DNA of the Toyota Production System and the core values of the Toyota Way. I have seen many who think about the TPS as a tool kit or lean manufacturing techniques that only work with Toyota because Toyota has a different process, a stable environment, or less fluctuation in customer demand. Others believe the TPS works only in the automotive industry.

Jeff K. Liker came out with a remarkable series of books starting with *The Toyota Way* (2003) and ending with *The Toyota Way to Lean Leadership* (Liker and Convis 2012). He revealed the real TPS based on his thirty-plus years of experience studying Toyota. It took him seven books to explain and decode the TPS. It is a Thinking Production System. It is neither a waste removal tool nor a lean manufacturing tactic. Liker presented very well the leadership model behind the system's success.

The TPS is really not what many think. So, what is TPS?

TPS Is a Thinking Production System

When a company says the TPS didn't work for them, it is a leadership failure. I suspect they tried to use the tools rigidly. The tools are flexible, adaptable, and implementable in many different conditions and industries. That's why you have to think about the tools and use your mind. Develop your people and motivate them to think and act.

TPS Is a Long-Term Innovation Process

Without innovation, Toyota would have never have succeeded in anything. Toyota's R&D department has played a major role in Toyota's success. For example, the Toyota wiring loom has gone through several major improvements and developments. The Toyota Prius was the first hybrid vehicle. *Minomi* is a revolution in the material movement. For those who don't know minomi, it is an innovation initiated in Japan. It is focused on eliminating containers completely. One of the Toyota companies in Japan (Central Motors) successfully created a revolution in material flow through a well-designed system to move parts without containers. The system is called minomi. The details are in *The Toyota Way to Lean Leadership* by Liker and Convis (2012).

TPS Is a Customizable Production System

The TPS system can't be copied. What has worked in one environment or specific industry might not work in another. Even from one Toyota plant to another, the system can't be copied identically. You have to think and adapt the tools. You must tailor them to your needs to suit the current conditions. The best example comes from the minomi system. When the Toyota plant in Georgetown, Kentucky, tried to copy and paste the technique from the Japanese plant, the process failed. Later, Gary Convis, the president of the Kentucky plant, led the implementation of the new method using the

Toyota Way. They had success because Gary was trained very well in lean thinking. This leads again to the first point. The TPS is a Thinking Production System. The real point is to make people think, and the system won't succeed without leaders trained on lean thinking and lean culture.

TPS Is a Productivity Improvement System

The TPS is not only for manufacturing. The TPS gives outstanding results in any area in which you want to achieve overall improvement in productivity, quality, safety, and reliability. It works very well with many different industries and businesses, and that includes health care, hotels, banking, construction, and more. The problem with the word "production" is that it makes many people think the system is for manufacturing. What about accelerating the check-in and check-out processes in a hotel? Won't this improve productivity and customer experience? There are many success stories outside of manufacturing industries presented in various lean references. However, people somehow managed to ignore the whole-system aspect of lean thinking and started calling it "lean" or "lean manufacturing" instead. This reduction in scope allowed business leaders to dismiss lean as a manufacturing idea. As a result, manufacturing companies believed lean could be delegated, and nonmanufacturing companies believed lean didn't apply to them at all.

TPS Is the Toyota Problem-Solving Routine

Yes, Toyota has its own unique way of solving problems and developing leaders. As mentioned in chapter "Embedding Improvement into the Daily Routine", Toyota has a psychology of process improvement unlike its competitors. Mike Rother (2009) in his Toyota Kata book tried to address what Toyota didn't document or address, and provides an excellent example of a good habitual routine that can lead to change behavior and overtime change culture.

The Deming cycle (PDCA) is a learning cycle rather than a process-improvement cycle. If you solve the problem but don't develop your people, the process will fail. People will not be able to continue managing the process in the new way if they haven't been trained in the culture of continuous improvement. Things will slip back, and it will be difficult to sustain the lean results. This is the problem in many companies.

TPS Is Toyota's People and Systems

People built, modified, and improved this system. People are the foundation of continuous improvement. People are more important than the process, and companies should give higher priority to developing their people and providing excellent working environments for them. Unfortunately, many companies say they do lean, Six Sigma, and other improvement projects to boost morale and develop new routines of thinking. However, they are actually focusing only on the processes and seeking quick outcomes. Toyota is highly committed to leadership development and training and coaching their employees. In *Toyota Under Fire* by Liker and Ogden (2010), when Liker interviewed Akio

Toyoda after several recall crises, Mr. Toyoda said the rate of growth had been higher than the rate of people development.

TPS Is a System to Build Quality for Customers

Jidoka is one of the main pillars of the TPS. The TPS is represented like a roof. Take away any of the pillars holding up the roof, and the system will collapse. Take out quality, and there is no TPS. Jidoka is a principle of building quality for customers—not inspecting quality. Building quality mean making it right the first time. If you are making defective products or using unacceptable quality standards and filtering these defects out through an inspection system, there is no building quality—and no jidoka. You are just catching the mistakes made in the manufacturing process. This costs a lot of money and resources and puts the business at risk if a defective product passes to the customer. Quality is what keeps any organization in business.

TPS Is a Strategy

The TPS is a strategy for excellence. The TPS is a strategy to achieve the goals of excellence in quality, productivity, costs, safety, and morale (Liker and Trachilis 2015). Without a vision aligned with the strategic objectives and stretch goals, the improvement effort will have no direction. The hoshin kanri process will help align the goals, plans, and efforts toward a common goal in order to achieve strategic business objectives. Hoshin kanri pays attention to the method rather than the results—unlike other traditional management approaches, such as MBO. Hoshin kanri focuses on innovative methods for achieving targets under a highly motivational developmental system.

TPS Is Total Performance Solutions

If used properly, these tools can turn around any organization. Speed kills competition. All the tools you need to maximize your productivity, quality, speed, and deliveries are included in the TPS. You just need to learn how to use these tools and implement the culture required to use them in your organization. Remember, a good culture will last forever. A good tool kit under a stressed management system will die quickly. It is all about leadership and how you are going to use these tools.

TPS Is Not Lean

Yes, people called it an inventory reduction program when they first heard of it. "Just in time" is one of the main pillars in the TPS. "Just in time" ideally means "one-piece flow." Inventory is the greatest waste in the process, and it hides many problems, such as quality problems, breakdown times, waiting waste, and more. Let's get back to history. Prior to the 1970 oil crisis, very few people in the world know what Toyota was up to. The fact that it emerged stronger than ever while many of its competitors were quite battered made people take notice. People went to Japan to find out how Toyota had done this. What people found was that Toyota was doing something called "just in time." In the West, this was interpreted as an inventory reduction program. As a result, it became known as the "just-in-time inventory" program. Nobody really believed inventory could be taken out of the whole value stream. Therefore, "just in time" came to mean "go beat the heck out of your suppliers." The big three auto companies (Ford, General Motors, and Chrysler) had lots of power over their suppliers, and they became pretty expert at this tactic—to their eventual detriment. James P. Womack came forward with *Lean Thinking* in 1996 and helped many to see the whole value chain. He showed how waste clogs the system and how continuous improvement was needed to link all parts of the chain to customer demand. He explained his findings in plain English, but once again people didn't hear. Lean might be an element of the larger strategy, but it is most likely to be relegated to plant and manufacturing work. As a result, one company after another has tried lean and failed.

TPS Is Not a Translated Production System

Many techniques used today (with awareness or not) have Japanese names. This includes techniques such as *poka yoke*, hoshin kanri, genchi genbutsu, and others.

The TPS is not a documented process. It can, therefore, be translated via people in Japan and the United States and passed through different cultures. Taiichi Ohno refused at the beginning to document the TPS for fear that people would narrowly focus on tools and theories. He said to write it would be to kill it. For example, "genchi genbutsu," or gemba, is translated as "go and see." Leaders, however, will only go and see when there is a problem. Gemba is being used only as a problem-solving process. As presented in chapter 2, gemba is a place for teaching and learning management. Gemba is the place where value-creating work happens and where you should put value for your customers. All lean tools and techniques, such as value stream mapping, work-standardization processes, and more, must be planned, measured, adapted, standardized, and improved at the workplace. Gemba is a place to solve problems by grasping the current situation and finding the root causes of problems by asking the five whys.

TPS Is a Pull System—Not a Kanban System

A pull system is the key to avoiding overproduction waste. You are linking the chain to customer demand instead of a schedule. You are no longer producing based on a schedule. As presented in *The Toyota Way*, kanban is an organized system of inventory buffers. According to Ohno, inventory is a waste, so kanban is something to strive to get rid of—not be proud of.

TPS Is Not Making to Order in Sequence

The TPS promotes leveling rather than making to order in sequence. Most suppliers try to follow the lean principle of making to order. However, since customer demands are never stable and are naturally unpredictable, irregular, and significantly varied, following the customer demand in sequence can cause a lot of issues and waste. You have to level the product volume and type. That's why many businesses have difficulties building to order. This is also why they say Toyota has a stable environment and less fluctuation in customer demand and why the TPS is only suitable for Toyota. They don't understand the underlying power of leveling.

TPS Is an Eight-Step Toyota Business Practice

There are eight steps in Toyota's business practice when solving problems. As mentioned earlier, Toyota uses PDCA as a routine for learning. The plan stage is invoked five times to ensure the root cause of the problem has been eliminated. Lean emphasizes the plan. The plan phase cannot be created without a daily observation at the gemba to find the root causes of problems, gather facts, discuss things with the process operators, and develop the best countermeasure from different alternatives.

TPS Is Not Zero Inventory

Many think just-in-time inventory means zero inventory. The ideal thing is one-piece flow, and this can only be established through a production cell. There is an inventory buffer, but it is not often used. There is a buffer in the Andon[1] system.

---

[1] The Andon system is a part of the Toyota principle of building quality for customers (jidoka) and refers to the use of

There is a buffer to protect your customer. There is a buffer to avoid stopping the whole production line to fix a problem. There is a buffer to avoid breaking down a critical manufacturing process.

TPS Is Built on Deep Supplier Relationships

This is one of the most important factors in Toyota's success. Few companies realize the importance of working with your suppliers to improve your own process and the value you provide to your customers. If you are not working with your suppliers to truly reduce inventory holdings, the process will fail. If you are trying to reduce inventory and ask your supplier to deliver smaller batch sizes more frequently, and if your supplier is not ready, the process will fail. I have seen many companies trying to shift the costs of holding inventory to their suppliers. This offers no real savings in the complete value stream! You are redistributing the cost to suppliers, but there

---

an alarm system on the production line to prevent defects from passing to the next process.

are no real savings. Very few people understand this. I recommend reading *Building Deep Supplier Relationships* from the Harvard Business Review (Liker and Choi 2004). Building these kinds of relations with suppliers is one of the most difficult parts of implementing the TPS, but it is also the most important part.

This book is not about explaining TPS in a few sentences. As I mentioned, it took Jeff K. Liker seven books to explain the real TPS. The purpose of these short sentences is to serve as a reminder. They are to provide you with just a specific level of awareness. You have to read more, practice, and perform real projects in order to gather in-depth knowledge.

Appendix II. Lean Resources

There are many books and articles written on lean leadership and management that this book cites. They are all listed at the end of the book and I also include additional recommended resources for further reading:

Borris, S. 2012. *Strategic Lean Mapping.* New York: McGraw-Hill.

Harris, R., C. Harris, and Earl Wilson. 2003. *Making Materials Flow: A Lean Material Handling Guide for Operations, Production-Control, and Engineering Professionals.* Cambridge, MA: Lean Enterprise Institute.

Liker, J. K., and K. J. Franz. 2011. *The Toyota Way to Continuous Improvement: Linking Strategy and Operational Excellence to Achieve Superior Performance.* New York: McGraw-Hill.

Rick Harris, Chris Harris, Earl Wilson, Jim Womack, Dan Jones, John Shook, Jose Ferro. 2003. *Making Materials Flow: A*

Lean Material-Handling Guide for Operations, Production-Control, and Engineering Professionals; version 1.0 Edition.

Rother, M., and R. Harris. 2001. *Creating Continuous Flow: An Action Guide for Managers, Engineers and Production Associates*. Cambridge, MA: Lean Enterprise Institute.

Shook, J. 2008. *Managing to Learn: Using the A3 Management Process to Solve Problems, Gain Agreement, Mentor and Lead.* Cambridge, MA: Lean Enterprise Institute.

Liker, J. K., Meier, D. (2005). Toyota Talent: *Developing Your People the Toyota Way*. New York: McGraw-Hill.

Soliman, M.H.A. (2016). *Hoshin Kanri: How Toyota Creates a Culture of Continuous Improvement to Achieve Lean Goals.* SC: CreateSpace.

Soliman, M. H. A. 2020. 5S: *A Practical Guide to Visualizing and Organizing Workplaces to Improve Productivity*. KDP.

Soliman, M. H. A. 2020. *Takt Time: A Guide to the Very Basic Lean Calculation*. KDP.

Soliman, M. H. A. 2020. *Kanban the Toyota Way: An Inventory Buffering System to Eliminate Inventory*. KDP.

Soliman, M. H. A. 2020. *Gemba Walks the Toyota Way: The Place to Teach and Learn Management*. KDP.

Soliman, M. H. A. 2020. *Jidoka: The Toyota Principle of Building Quality into the Process*. KDP.

Soliman, M. H. A. 2018. *Healthcare is Ripe for Lean*. Industrial Management.

References

Ahmed, M.H. (2014). Daily Walks Train Future Leaders. Industrial Management 56 (1): 22–27.
Google Scholar

Ahmed, M.H. (2013). Lean Transformation Guidance: Why Organizations Fail to Achieve and Sustain Excellence through Lean Improvement. International Journal of Lean Thinking 4 (1): 31–40.
Google Scholar

Balle, M. and Balle, F. (2014) Lead with Respect: A Novel of Lean Practice, Lean Enterprise Institute, Cambridge.

Balle, M. and Balle, F. (2010) Lean Manager: A Novel of Lean Transformation. Lean Enterprise Institute, Cambridge.

Byrne, A. (2012) The Lean Turnaround: How Business Leaders Use Lean Principles to Create Value and Transform Their Company. McGraw-Hill, New York.

Drucker, P. F. (1954). The Practice of management. New York: HarperCollins Publishers.

Kaufman, J. (2012) The Personal MBA: Master the Art of Business, Portfolio Publishing, New York.

Taylor, F. W. (1911). The principles of scientific management. New York: Harper & Brothers.

Liker, J. K., & Convis, G. L. (2012). Toyota way to lean leadership: Achieving and sustaining excellence through leadership development. New York: MacGraw-hill.

Liker, J. K. (2002) The Toyota Way: 14 Management Principles from the World's Greatest Manufacturer, McGraw-Hill, New York.

Rother, M. (2009). Toyota Kata: Managing People For Improvement, Adaptiveness, And Superior Results. New York: Macgraw-Hill.

Roy F. Baumeister and Brad J. Bushman. 2020. Social psychology and human nature. Cengage Learning.

Soliman, M.H.A. (2016) Hoshin Kanri. How Toyota Creates a Culture of Continuous Improvement to Achieve Lean Goals, CreateSpace, South Carolina.

Liker, J. K. and Trachilis, G. (2015) Developing Lean Leaders at All Levels: A Practical Guide, Lean Leadership Institute Publications, Cambridge.

Liker, J. K., Convis, G. L. (2012). Toyota Way to Lean Leadership: Achieving and Sustaining Excellence through Leadership Development. New York: Macgraw-Hill.

Liker, J. K., Trachilis, G. (2015). Developing Lean Leaders at All Levels: A Practical Guide. Cambridge, MA: Lean Leadership Institute Publications.

Liker, J. K., Meier, D. (2005). Toyota Talent: Developing Your People the Toyota Way. New York: McGraw-Hill.

Rother, M. (2009). Toyota Kata: Managing People for Improvement, Adaptiveness, And Superior Results. New York: Macgraw-Hill.

Shook. J. (2008). Managing to Learn: Using the A3 Management Process to Solve Problems, Gain Agreement, Mentor and Lead. Cambridge, MA: Lean Enterprise Institute.

Soliman, M.H.A. (2016). Hoshin Kanri: How Toyota Creates a Culture of Continuous Improvement to Achieve Lean Goals. SC: CreateSpace.
Google Scholar

Soliman, M.H.A. (2015). A New Routine for Culture Change. Industrial Management 57 (3): 25–30.
Google Scholar

Soliman, M.H.A. (2015). What Toyota Production System Is Really About? Unpublished. https://www.researchgate.net/publication/280557330_What_Toyota_Production_System_is_Really_About

Soliman, M. H. A. (2020). The Toyota Way to Effective Strategy Deployment: How Organizations Can Focus Energy on Key Priorities Through Hoshin Kanri to Achieve the Business Goals. Journal of Operations and Strategic Planning 3(1), 1-27. Sage Publications. DOI: https://doi.org/10.1177/2516600X20946542
Google Scholar

Soliman, M. H. A. (2017). Why Continuous Improvement Programs Fail in the Egyptian Manufacturing Organizations? A Research Study of the Evidence. AJIBM 7(3).
Google Scholar

Soliman, M. H. A. (2017). A COMPREHENSIVE REVIEW OF MANUFACTURING WASTES: TOYOTA PRODUCTION SYSTEM LEAN PRINCIPLES. EJER 22(2), 1-10.
Google Scholar

Soliman, M. H. A. 2020. Gemba Walks the Toyota Way: The Place to Teach and Learn Management. KDP.
ResearchGate

Soliman, M. H. A. 2020. 5S: A Practical Guide to Visualizing and Organizing Workplaces to Improve Productivity.
ResearchGate

Soliman, M. H. A. 2020. Takt Time: A Guide to the Very Basic Lean Calculation. KDP.
ResearchGate

Soliman, M. H. A. 2020. Kanban the Toyota Way: An Inventory Buffering System to Eliminate Inventory. KDP.
SSRN

Soliman, M. H. A. 2015. Developing People Improves the Process. Industrial Management 58(1).
Google Scholar

Soliman, M. H. A. 2020. Turning PDCA into a Routine for Learning. KDP.

Soliman, M. H. A. 2020. Lean Accounting: Why Accounting Department Should Switch to Lean. KDP.

About the Author

Mohammed Hamed Ahmed Soliman is an industrial engineer, consultant, university lecturer, operational excellence leader, and author. He works as a lecturer at the American University in Cairo and as a consultant for several international industrial organizations.

Soliman earned a bachelor of science in Engineering and a master's degree in Quality Management. He earned post-graduate degrees in Industrial Engineering and Engineering Management. He holds numerous certificates in management, industry, quality, and cost engineering.

For most of his career, Soliman worked as a regular employee for various industrial sectors. This included crystal-glass making, fertilizers, and chemicals. He did this while educating people about the culture of continuous improvement.

Soliman has lectured at Princess Noura University and trained the maintenance team in Vale Oman Pelletizing Company. He has been lecturing at The American University in Cairo for 6 year and has designed and delivered 40 leadership and technical skills enhancement training modules.

Soliman is a member at the Institute of Industrial and Systems Engineers and a member with the Society for Engineering and Management Systems. He has published several articles in peer reviewed academic journals and magazines. His writings on lean manufacturing, leadership, productivity, and business appear in Industrial Engineers, Lean Thinking, and Industrial Management. Soliman's blog is www.personal-lean.org.

Also by Mohammed Hamed Ahmed Soliman

https://www.amazon.com/-/e/B00NEY7BRE?fbclid=IwAR1ZM31VKzUyiytw5hKuzu3c9btnuPn08JOb2oA4PWE8h26G_jdG9Cqn2Ag

www.ingramcontent.com/pod-product-compliance
Lightning Source LLC
Chambersburg PA
CBHW020434220526
45464CB00002B/696